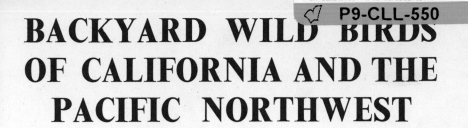

BACKYARD WILD BIRDS
OF CALIFORNIA AND THE
PACIFIC NORTHWEST

By Vinson Brown

Illustrated by Rosinda Holmes

Published by T.F.H. Publications, Inc., TFH Building, 245 Cornelison Avenue, Jersey
City, N. J. 07302. Distributed in the British Empire by T.F.H. Publications (London),
Ltd., 13 Nutley Lane, Reigate, Surrey, England. In Canada, to the Pet Trade by
Canadian Aquarium Supply Co. and Viobin of 1125 Talbot Street, St. Thomas,
Ontario, Canada. In Canada, to the Book Trade, by Clarke, Irwin & Company
Limited, Clarwin House, 791 St. Clair Avenue West, Toronto 10, Ontario, Canada.
Printed in the U.S.A. by the lithograph process by T.F.H. Lithograph Corp., Jersey
City, N. J. 07302.

INTRODUCTION

The main purpose of this book is to give the user a handy, reasonably priced guide to the common birds found in backyards of the coast from California to British Columbia and west of the crests of the Cascades and Sierras. The book shows how such birds may be attracted to these yards for greater enjoyment. However, the book also describes and illustrates a number of less common land birds so that you may travel even into the high mountains, for example, and still use this book to help you in bird identification. Thus, this book becomes a fairly complete volume on the land birds of the Pacific Coast. One shore bird is included in the book, the killdeer, because it is often seen on large lawns.

To use the book, first learn to find bird types by shape in the helpful key on pages 6 and 7. The numbers in this key refer to numbered bird illustrations instead of page numbers. Carefully study these key pages so you can picture the shapes of the bodies, heads, wings, bills and tails of the various birds. Notice that some types of birds, such as the owls and wrens have thick bodies, others thin or medium bodies. Hawks are best differentiated by carefully studying the wing and tail shapes. Long, thin bills are distinctive of the thrashers and mockingbirds, while short, stout bills are typical of the sparrows and finches, general type bills are found among thrushes, blackbirds and orioles, who eat many kinds of foods, and short thin bills are typical of warblers, gnatcatchers and kinglets.

The book is built around the color plates in the back half and the line drawings in the front half for ease of use by beginners, and so is arranged somewhat differently than most bird books. The birds are kept, so far as possible, in their natural groups. Where a bird family, such as the flycatchers, are divided between the color plate section and the line drawing section of the book, the birds in the other section are mentioned by number in the section at which you are looking. Check these numbers, and the illustrations and descriptions to which they refer, carefully so you can picture in your mind the complete family of birds in your region.

♂ means male. ♀ means female.

ATTRACTING, FEEDING AND HOUSING BIRDS

Attracting birds to your backyard successfully requires: 1. providing them with habitats and hiding places that they like; 2. giving them favorite food plants; 3. putting up feeding and watering stations; 4. providing them with good nesting sites.

HABITATS AND HIDING PLACES. Produce in your yard a variety of places (habitats) in which birds like to live and hide. A grassy place, a little pond with rushes around it, trees, clusters of bushes, rough hedges, a vine-covered fence or wall, all are good.

FOOD PLANTS. Good *trees* and *shrubs* include elderberries, white mulberry, blueberry, flowering crab, red cedar, nanny berry, barberry, coralberry, smooth sumace, Japanese yew, peppertree, and Asiatic sweetleaf.

Good *vines* include Virginia creeper, greenbrier, honeysuckles (especially good for hummingbirds), grapes, and matrimony vines.

Useful *herbs* are sunflowers, chicory, blazing star, and asters. Ask about these and other plants birds like at your neighborhood nursery.

FEEDING AND WATERING STATIONS. Some of these are illustrated on the opposite page. Be sure all are protected from cats and squirrels by metal sheets tacked around trunks or poles, or by hanging from wires. Attract birds first by putting food on stumps and rocks, later luring them to stands and cable trays. Favorite foods of birds are listed in the descriptions. Many, including bird seed, suet and insect mixes, can be obtained at pet stores. Hummingbird nectar feeders are also obtainable at pet stores.

GOOD NESTING SITES. Natural nesting sites you furnish by providing trees, hedges, vines, brush, rushes and clumps of high grass. Five general types of homes for birds are shown on the opposite page. Home preferences where known for each bird are given in the bird descriptions. You will be disappointed about birds using your bird houses unless you carefully watch where each kind of bird likes to live and place your bird house where that bird likes it to be. Rustic bird houses that look like tree stumps are especially good. Notice that most holes are placed high on the house with a resting place just below. Some birds, such as the swallows and martins, nest in groups. A line of hollow gourds, with proper size holes, hung from a beam, wire or branch are good for these.

The illustrations on page 5 are from HOW TO MAKE A MINIATURE ZOO, by Vinson Brown, published by Little, Brown and Co., Boston, Massachusetts.

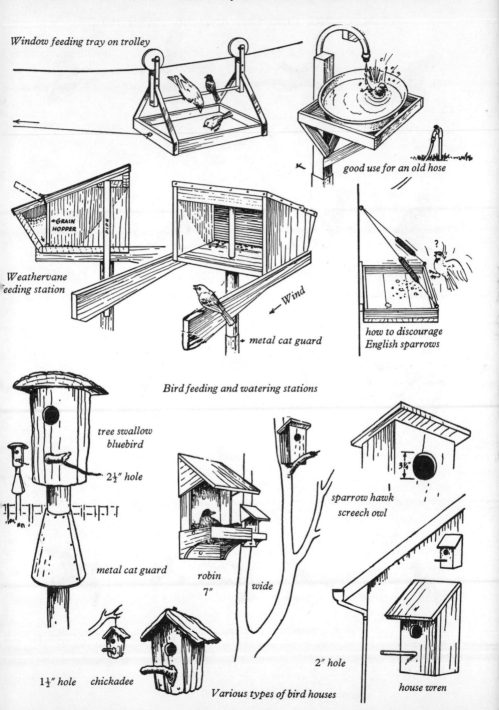

Window feeding tray on trolley

good use for an old hose

Weathervane feeding station

Wind

metal cat guard

how to discourage English sparrows

GRAIN HOPPER

PIPE

Bird feeding and watering stations

tree swallow
bluebird

2½" hole

metal cat guard

robin
7"

wide

sparrow hawk
screech owl

1½" hole   chickadee

2" hole

Various types of bird houses

house wren

KEY TO BIRD SHAPES

Soaring Hawks, 8-11
Vultures, 1

Marsh Hawk, 6
Osprey, 7

Falcons, 12-15
Kite, 2

Accipiter Hawks, 4- 5

Quail, 19-20
Grouse, 16-18
Chukar, p. 13

Pheasant, 21

Doves, 100-103
Pigeon, 99

Killdeer, 22

Nighthawks, 37-38   Owls, 23-34

Woodpeckers,
110-122

Kingfisher, 42

Hummingbirds,
104-109

Kingbirds,
124-126
Flycatchers,
44-49, 123

Roadrunner,
35

Swallows,
51-57

Swifts,
39-41

Poorwill,
36

Yellow-billed Cuckoo, 43

KEY TO BIRD SHAPES

Magpies, 58

Crows, 59-60
Nutcracker, 61

Jays, 131-133

Shrikes, 129-130

Thrushes, 142-144
Robin, 141
Bluebirds, 139-140
Solitaire, 76

Horned Lark, 50

Chickadees, 62, 134
Titmouse, 63

Thrashers, 73-74-75
Mockingbird, 72

Nuthatches, 135-137
Creeper, 138

Wrens, 67-71

Bushtit, 64

Wren-tit, 65

Warblers, 149-160
Kinglets, 127-128
Vireos, 79-82

Gnatcatchers, 77-78

Waxwings, 145-146
Phainopepla, 147

Orioles, 165-166
Meadowlarks, 161
Blackbirds, 85-86;
162-164

Crossbill, 177
Grosbeaks,
169-172
Tanagers, 167
Cardinal, 168

Goldfinches, 178-181
Purple Finches,
173-175

Juncos, 98
Sparrows, 87-97
Bunting, 176
Towhees, 182-184

1. TURKEY VULTURE

2. WHITE-TAILED KITE

3. GOSHAWK
adult

4. SHARP-SHINNED HAWK

immature

5. COOPER'S HAWK

6. MARSH HAWK
♂

7. OSPREY

VULTURES, KITE, BIRD HAWKS, MARSH HAWK AND OSPREY

VULTURES, KITE, BIRD HAWKS, MARSH HAWK AND OSPREY

All birds described here and on page 11 are meat or fish eaters. Some may be attracted by tying nets with fresh meat in them on branches.

1. TURKEY VULTURE (*Cathartes aura*). Wingspread 6′. Resident in southern California; summer visitor north to British Columbia. Found mainly in open areas and cliffs, but also in forest openings. *Black body; black wings ashy-gray on the hind borders; neck and head naked red.* Feeds on carrion. Often seen soaring. The related CALIFORNIA CONDOR (*Gymnogyps californianus*), of southern California, has a 9′ wingspread and white area under black wings. Rare.

2. WHITE-TAILED KITE (*Elanus leucurus*). Wingspread 2½′; length 15-17″. Resident from Sonoma County and Sacramento Valley south. Found mainly along streams, marshes and in open areas. *Generally white with gray and black markings.* Often hovers.

3. GOSHAWK (*Accipiter gentilis*). Wingspread 3½′; length 21-24″. Resident in high mountain forests of west and northern wilderness; winter visitor in nearby lowlands; almost always in woods. *Black cap marked off by white line above eye is distinctive;* upper parts bluish-gray; light gray beneath. A fierce killer of birds.

4. SHARP-SHINNED HAWK (*Accipiter striatus*). Length 10-14″. Resident in forest and woods of most of area except higher peaks; migrant and winter visitor in southern California. Blackish head: body bluish-gray above, white and reddish-brown below; *square-tipped tail.*

5. COOPER'S HAWK (*Accipiter cooperi*). Length 14-20″. Same as Sharp-shinned Hawk in residence and appearance, but larger and the *longer tail is round-tipped.* Both sneak through brush and trees to capture birds.

6. MARSH HAWK (*Circus cyaneus*). Wingspread 3½-4½′; length 17-24″. Common summer visitor in marshlands, grasslands and cultivated areas. *Distinctive white rump;* male bluish-gray above, female brown. Harries prey by diving and swooping.

7. OSPREY (*Pandion haliaetus*). Wingspread 4½-6′; length 22-26″. Summer visitor and migrant along coast and at lakes. *Large size and brown-marked whitish head are distinctive;* dark brown body above. Dives into water to catch fish.

Buteos-flight silhouette

8. RED-TAILED HAWK

9. SWAINSON'S HAWK

11. RED-SHOULDERED HAWK

10. ROUGH-LEGGED HAWK

Falcons-flight silhouette

13. PIGEON HAWK

12. SPARROW HAWK

15. PEREGRINE FALCON

14. PRAIRIE FALCON

Rh

EAGLES, SOARING HAWKS AND FALCONS

EAGLES, SOARING HAWKS AND FALCONS

The rare GOLDEN EAGLE and BALD EAGLE (not illustrated) have wingspreads of 6-8′. The adult Golden is golden-brown; the adult Bald Eagle has a white head and tail.

8. RED-TAILED HAWK (*Buteo jamaicensis*). Wingspread 4-4½′; length 19-25″. Resident in most of lower elevations in cliffs and over open areas and brushlands; some summer in clearings of high mountains. *Bright red rounded tail in adult*; immature has light gray tail with numerous black bars; general color is streaked brownish.

9. SWAINSON'S HAWK (*Buteo swainsoni*). Wingspread 4-4½′; length 19-23″. Breeds in cliffs and soars over more open areas; rare in forests; rare in winter in south. *Has clear yellow underwing and narrow bands on light gray tail.*

10. ROUGH-LEGGED HAWK (*Buteo lagopus*). Wingspread 4-4½′; length 20-24″. Winters in open areas in most of region except southern California. Body usually blackish-brown beneath (some have light bellies); *black patch on underside of wing.*

11. RED-SHOULDERED HAWK (*Buteo lineatus*). Wingspread 3-4′; length 18-22″. Resident in California, mainly in open woodland along lowland rivers. *Under-parts reddish-brown*; brownish above; chestnut on wingbend; *white bars on black tail.*

12. SPARROW HAWK (*Falco sparverius*). Wingspread 1-1½′; length 9-12″. Resident in most of our region in open areas, open woods, parks and backyard trees. *Rufous back and tail distinctive*; bluish wings and crown. Often hovers. Attract to sparrow-hawk type house; likes suet and meat scraps.

13. PIGEON HAWK (*Falco columbarius*). Wingspread 1-1½′; length 11-13″. Breeds from British Columbia to Oregon; winters in lowlands and south; in open woodland, marshes and open country. Bluish-gray general color; streaked below; *very long wings.*

14. PRAIRIE FALCON (*Falco mexicanus*). Wingspread 3½′; length 15-21″. Resident in much of region in dry canyons and open areas. Pale brownish-colored; *black patches at base of wings contrast sharply with whitish wings.*

15. PEREGRINE FALCON (*Falco peregrinus*). Wingspread 3½′; length 15-21″. Resident in most of area, but rare in southern California in summer; mainly lives in cliffs, marshes and open country. *Distinctive dark stripe down each side of head*; whitish beneath with narrow dark bars. Extremely swift, often catching ducks in flight.

17. RUFFED GROUSE

16. BLUE GROUSE

18. WHITE-TAILED
PTARMIGAN

20. MOUNTAIN QUAIL

19. CALIFORNIA QUAIL

21. RING-NECKED PHEASANT

22. KILLDEER

Rh

GROUSE, PTARMIGAN, QUAIL, PHEASANT AND KILLDEER

GROUSE, PTARMIGAN, QUAIL, PHEASANT AND KILLDEER

As plant (except killdeer) and insect eaters, the following birds may often be attracted by grain, birdseed, suet and insect mixes put low in bushes, or among grasses.

16. BLUE GROUSE (*Dendragapus obscurus*). Length 16-19″. Resident in coniferous forests and burns as far south as Mount Pinos, California. *Tail blackish with broad light-gray band at tip*; male dark gray; female brownish. Likes fir seeds, berries, etc. Male makes hollow, hooting sound; both sexes give loud **"kuk-kuk-kuk!"**

17. RUFFED GROUSE (*Dendragapus obscurus*). Length 16-19″. Resident in hardwood forests or mixed hardwood and coniferous forests from British Columbia to northwest California. *Broad black band near tip of tail; reddish-brown above*; yellow-brown below. Male makes loud booming sound with wings. Likes berries, cherries and clover.

18. WHITE-TAILED PTARMIGAN (*Lagopus leucurus*). Length 12-13″. Resident in British Columbia and Cascade Mountains of northern Washington in open places; lower in winter. *Distinctive white tail*; brown with white belly and wings in summer; white in winter.

19. CALIFORNIA QUAIL (*Lophortyx californicus*). Length 9-11″. Resident from southern Oregon south in grasslands and broken chaparral, oak woods, streamside woods and parks, and cultivated areas. General bluish-gray color above; buffy below. Black plume curves forward from crown; male with white-circled black throat. Rallying cry of **"quer-ca-go!"**

20. MOUNTAIN QUAIL (*Oreortyx pictus*). Length 10-13″. Resident from northern Washington south mainly in brushy mountain slopes and brush mixed with forest. The *reddish-brown throat and long straight plume are distinctive*; general color bluish-gray. A loud, resonant **"t-wook!"** or **"ti-yoork"** cry. Likes lupin and clover seed.

The CHUKAR (not illustrated), a 12-14″ long, gray and reddish-brown partridge-like bird should be mentioned here. It is found in drier valleys and mountain slopes in grass and brush.

21. RING-NECKED PHEASANT (*Phasianus colchicus*). Length 20-33″. Introduced resident in irrigated land and farm grain land of our region. *The long pointed tail of both sexes is distinctive*; male brilliantly colored; female mottled brown. Likes barley and wheat seeds.

22. KILLDEER (*Charadrius vociferus*). Length 10-11″. Resident in grasslands, riverbanks, gardens, parks, irrigated lands and lawns. *The golden-red rump and the two black bands on breast are distinctive.* **"Kee-dee-dee"** shrill cry. Likes live insects and worms.

23. BARN OWL

26. GREAT HORNED OWL

28. GREAT GRAY OWL

25. FLAMMULATED OWL

27. SNOWY OWL

24. SCREECH OWL

OWLS

OWLS

Most owls fly by night and are live meat eaters. Smaller owls sometimes nest in a bird house of hollow-log type, sparrow-hawk size.

23. BARN OWL (*Tyto alba*). 15-18″. Common resident in cliffs, open areas, open woodlands, buildings and parks. *The heart-shaped, monkey-like face and the yellowish-brown and white color are distinctive.* It has a soft, moth-like flight, and gives a high-pitched snore-hiss when disturbed.

24. SCREECH OWL (*Otus asio*). Length 8-10″. Resident in most of our region in open woodlands, coastal coniferous forest, along streams, in buildings and in yards with trees and cultivated land. *The only small gray owl with big ear tufts,* though may appear in reddish color phase; black streaks on body. Tremulous whistle.

25. FLAMMULATED OWL (*Otus flammeolus*). 6-7″. Summer visitor in mountain coniferous forests. *Short ears and small size* distinguish this owl from the screech owl, as do the *distinctive brown eyes.* It has a steadily repeated mellow hoot at a low pitch.

26. GREAT HORNED OWL (*Bubo virginianus*). 18-25″. Widespread common resident in hardwoods and coniferous forests, cliffs, grass, brush and cultivated areas. *The only very large owl with ear tufts or "horns," the "horns" being far apart on head.* Dark brown or blackish above; thick body. Deep **"hoo-hoo, hoo-hoo"** cry.

27. SNOWY OWL (*Nyctea scandiaca*). Length 21-26″. Occasional winter visitor as far south as northern California in mountains, in grassy and cultivated areas, marshes and along seashore. *White all over,* but marked with black above; black bill and yellow eyes. It often hunts by day and may perch on hay stacks, posts, dunes, etc. Usually silent.

28. GREAT GRAY OWL (*Strix nebulosa*). 25-32″. Resident as far south as central California, mainly in mountain and sub-alpine coniferous forests. *It is the largest of our owls with a 5 foot wingspread;* dark brown above, marked with grayish-white; light gray breast streaked with dark brown. Deep, echoing **"Hooo!"**

31. SPOTTED OWL

34. SAW-WHET OWL

32. LONG-EARED OWL

29. PYGMY OWL

33. SHORT-EARED OWL

30. BURROWING OWL

36. POOR WILL

35. ROADRUNNER

OWLS, ROADRUNNER AND POOR WILL

29. PYGMY OWL (*Glaucidium gnoma*), 7-7½″. Common resident of coniferous forest and mixed hardwood-conifers; mainly in mountains in California. Small gray-brown or red-brown owl *with narrow black breast stripes*. Soft, whistled **"tewk-tew-kew"** call, often rapidly repeated.

30. BURROWING OWL (*Speotyto cunicularia*). 9-11″. Breeds through most of our region, but leaves cold areas in winter; mainly lives in grasslands. Brown with light markings; *very long legs for an owl*; white line over eye. Often flies in daylight and usually lights at ground squirrel holes. Chuckles or gives soft **"cooo-hooo."**

31. SPOTTED OWL (*Strix occidentalis*). 18-19″. Common resident of coniferous forests along coast and in mountains; also oak trees, especially in winter. A large dark brown and earless owl with *many white spots on upper sides*; face yellowish-brown. Barks, or gives high pitched **"whoo-hoo-hoooo"** or whistle-like **"wheeee."**

32. LONG-EARED OWL (*Asio otus*). 14-16″. Breeds over most of region in oak and river woods and grasslands; moves south from colder country in winter. *"Horns" very close together, conspicuous and narrow*; grayish body; reddish-brown face. Whines, mews or gives soft **"coo."**

33. SHORT-EARED OWL (*Asio flammeus*). 14-17″. Resident in most of region in marshes, grasslands, irrigated land, etc. *Ear tufts very short and black*; pale patches show on wings in flight; yellow-brown color. Floppy swooping flight, sometimes by day. Has loud, nasal **"tee-yow!"**

34. SAW-WHET OWL (*Aegolius acadicus*). 7-8″. Resident in mountains and sub-alpine coniferous forests and oaks as far south as southern California mountains. *Small brown owl with wide brown markings on light colored undersides*; white spots on wings. Saw-like call.

35. ROADRUNNER (*Geococcyx californianus*). 20-24″. Resident from north central California south, mainly in desert, chaparral and oak areas. A large gray-brownish streaked bird *with long pointed tail and powerful legs*. Loud **"coo"** call, also rattling note. An insect and reptile eater.

36. POOR WILL (*Phalaenoptilus nuttallii*). 7-8″. Breeds from British Columbia south in brushlands, rocky cliffs and oaks; winters from central California south; appears mainly at night. General gray-brown colors; *dark marked outer tail feathers white-tipped*. Soft **"poo-woo"** call. Insect eater.

41. WHITE-THROATED SWIFT

39. BLACK SWIFT

40. VAUX'S SWIFT

38. LESSER NIGHTHAWK

37. COMMON NIGHTHAWK

42. BELTED KINGFISHER

NIGHTHAWKS, SWIFTS AND KINGFISHER

NIGHTHAWKS, SWIFTS AND KINGFISHER

Both nighthawks and swifts usually catch insects on the wing, the swifts very high. Nighthawks work both in daylight and dusk, sleeping in a tree or in bushes, while swifts rest on high cliffs and fly by day. The very rapid "twinkling" flight of the swifts, sailing between spurts, is unlike the more steady flight of the swallows (see page 23).

37. COMMON NIGHTHAWK (*Chordeiles minor*). 8-10". Common summer visitor in high mountains and on northwest coast from Sonoma County, California, north in coniferous forest clearings and treeless plains; migrant in most areas. *Streaked brownish-gray; long narrow wings marked below by white or yellow-brown bar near tip.* Usually flies higher than tree-tops; makes booming noise after dive; also has nasal **"pee-ent"** call.

38. LESSER NIGHTHAWK (*Chordeiles acutipennis*). 8-9". Summer visitor from central California south in open areas. Similar to above bird, but *wing bars nearer tips of wings*. Also flies usually below treetops, and has mewing **"waa-waa-woo"** note.

39. BLACK SWIFT (*Cypseloides niger*). 7-8". Uncommon summer visitor from British Columbia to central California coast. Sierras and southern California mountains, on cliffs and in forests. *All black color and slightly forked tail are distinctive.* Might be mistaken for purple martin, but swift seldom lights on twig or wire like martin. Twitters.

40. VAUX'S SWIFT (*Chaetura vauxi*). 4-5". Common summer visitor in wooded, brushy and cultivated areas from British Columbia south to central California; migrant elsewhere. General color brownish-black; brown on rump and tail; *ashy on belly*. **"Chip-chip"** call.

41. WHITE-THROATED SWIFT (*Aeronautes saxatalis*). 6-7". Summer visitor from British Columbia south, mostly in mountain regions and not along humid coast; in cliffs, brush, oaks, cultivated and grassy areas. *White on flanks, middle of breast and throat; black elsewhere.* Shrill, twittering, **"jee-jee-jee-jee"** call.

42. BELTED KINGFISHER (*Megaceryle alcyon*). 11-14". Resident in lowlands near water; summer visitor along mountain streams and lakes. *bluish-gray above, white below; bushy crest*; white collar around neck; stout bill; large head. Dives and catches small fish. Loud, rattling cry.

43. YELLOW-BILLED CUCKOO

44. ASH-THROATED FLYCATCHER

45. BLACK PHOEBE

48. WESTERN WOOD PEEWEE

46. SAY'S PHOEBE

47. WESTERN FLYCATCHER

49. OLIVE-SIDED FLYCATCHER

50. HORNED LARK

Rh

CUCKOO, FLYCATCHERS AND HORNED LARK

CUCKOO, FLYCATCHERS AND HORNED LARK

With the exception of the horned lark, which also eats seeds, all birds on this page are insect eaters. Robin-type bird-houses of proportionate size are favored by flycatchers and probably by cuckoo. (For other flycatchers, see numbers 123-126).

43. YELLOW-BILLED CUCKOO (*Coccyzus americanus*). 12½-13½″. Summer visitor along large wooded streams. Brown above, white below; *three outer black tail feathers have large white spots*. Explosive **"kak-kak, kow, keow!"**

44. ASH-THROATED FLYCATCHER (*Myiarchus cinerascens*). 8-8½″. Common summer visitor near water in wooded areas, also in grasslands, brush, orchards and parks. *Reddish-brown tail*; dark back; *two white wing bars*; white belly. **"Prrrt"** and **"key-whirr"** calls.

45. BLACK PHOEBE (*Sayornis nigricans*). 6½-7″. Common resident in most of low country in cliffs, buildings, streamside woods and cultivated land. *All black except white belly*; immature bird brownish-black and white. **"Fee-bee!"** call. Likes to nest under roof ledge.

46. SAY'S PHOEBE (*Sayornis saya*). 7-8″. Resident from central California south; migrant and summer visitor in northern-most California; in cliffs, buildings and open places. *Dark to grayish-brown above, reddish-brown beneath, except gray throat*. **"Phee-ee"** call.

All *Empidonax* flycatchers (see below) look very much alike.

47. WESTERN FLYCATCHER (*Empidonax difficilis*). Common summer visitor *near water in wooded areas*. Body above olive-brown, yellow beneath; white eye ring; two white wing bars. *Wheezy note with rising inflection*. TRAILL'S FLYCATCHER (*Empidonax traillii*), similar, but lives in willow thickets and has *sneeze-call like*. HAMMOND'S FLYCATCHER (*Empidonax hammondii*), similar, but *lives in brushlands with scattered trees*. GRAY FLY-CATCHER (*Empidonax wrightii*), similar, but lives in southern California willow and cottonwood thickets and has **"chee-weep"** call.

48. WESTERN WOOD PEEWEE (*Contopus sordidulus*). 6-6½″. Common summer visitor in wooded areas. *Plain dark, olive-gray-brown bird with no white eye ring*. Nasal **"pee-wee"** call.

49. OLIVE-SIDED FLYCATCHER (*Nuttallornis borealis*). 7-8″. Common summer visitor to wooded areas. *Two dark chest patches, separated by white center stripe*. **"Pee-fsee"** or **"pee-pee-pah"** cry.

50. HORNED LARK (*Eremophila alpestris*). 7-8″. Resident in drier, open areas, also in park, farms and ranches. *Black collar, yellow throat and "horns" are distinctive*. Shrill **"szee"** or **"tsee-dee-ree"** call. Likes bird seed.

51. VIOLET-GREEN
SWALLOW

52. TREE SWALLOW

53. BANK SWALLOW

54. ROUGH-WINGED
SWALLOW

55. BARN SWALLOW

56. CLIFF SWALLOW

♂

57. PURPLE MARTIN

♀

SWALLOWS AND MARTINS

SWALLOWS AND MARTINS

Swallows are almost entirely insect-eaters, catching bugs on the wing.

51. VIOLET-GREEN SWALLOW (*Tachycineta thalassina*). 5-5½". Abundant migrant and summer visitor in wooded and low mountain areas; also in grasslands, towns, cliffs, and brush; winter visitor in southern California. *Iridescent bronze, green, purple and violet above; white on sides of face and rump.* Sometimes will nest in blue-bird-size houses under eaves of buildings. Gives two to three weak **"tseep"** notes.

52. TREE SWALLOW (*Iridoprocne bicolor*). 5-6". Common summer visitor and migrant in wooded and grassy areas, mainly interior and near water. *Male bright green or blue-black above, bright white below;* female and immature are brown above. **"Keely-keely-tsee-tee-keely"** call. Nests in trees, but also in blue-bird-size houses placed on posts in open.

53. BANK SWALLOW (*Riparia riparia*). 5-5½". Migrant and summer visitor, making nests in banks near streams or lakes; flies over grasslands. *Dark band across white breast.* Soft **"brrrt"** note.

54. ROUGH-WINGED SWALLOW (*Stelgidopteryx ruficollis*). 5-6". Common summer visitor and migrant in open areas near water. Brown above; *breast and throat brownish-gray.* Weak **"preet"** call. Also nests in colonies in banks.

55. BARN SWALLOW (*Hirundo rustica*). 6-7½". Common migrant and summer visitor, mainly in lower, open country, near water and buildings, from Bakersfield north, rarer in south. *Orange-brown below and on forehead; forked tail.* Twittering cry, or sharp **"tee-keet"** or **"eet-eet."** Builds open mud nests and will occasionally live in groups of robin-like bird houses placed under eaves of buildings.

56. CLIFF SWALLOW (*Petrochelidon pyrrhonota*). 5-6". Abundant summer visitor and migrant in open areas, especially near water, cliffs and buildings. Builds gourd-shaped clay or mud nests. *Rump is pale, orange-brown; upper parts steely-blue.* **"Kyeer-kyeer"** alarm note, or low **"chrrrr."**

57. PURPLE MARTIN (*Progne subis*). 8-9". Irregular summer visitor in colonies among woodlands in low mountains or edges of cities and on farms. *Male blue-black all over;* female brown above and whitish belly. Put up rows of hollow gourd bird houses, hung in open 10-12′ above ground, each with hole about 2½″ wide, to attract colony. Deep, harmonious song ends in gutteral trill.

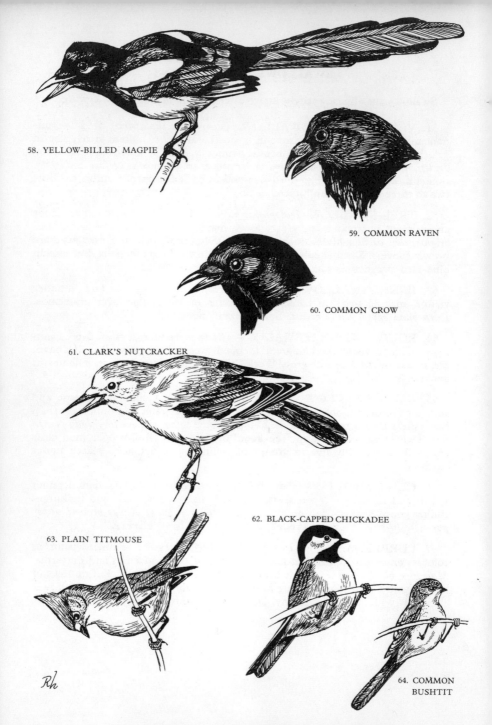

58. YELLOW-BILLED MAGPIE

59. COMMON RAVEN

60. COMMON CROW

61. CLARK'S NUTCRACKER

63. PLAIN TITMOUSE

62. BLACK-CAPPED CHICKADEE

64. COMMON BUSHTIT

Rh

MAGPIES, CROWS, CHICKADEE, TITMOUSE AND BUSHTIT

MAGPIES, CROWS, CHICKADEE, TITMOUSE AND BUSHTIT

58. YELLOW-BILLED MAGPIE (*Pica nuttalli*). 17-22″. Resident in central Californian valleys from Ventura County north to San Francisco and Redding. *Large black and white bird with very long tail and yellow bill.* Nasal, querulous **"maag"** call. Omnivorous feeder, including carrion. Suet placed in low trees will attract it; also bird seed, figs and grapes.

59. COMMON RAVEN (*Corvus corax*). 21-27″. Common resident in cliffs and open areas, especially near sea. Black all over like crow, but with *very rough-looking throat feathers; tail wedge-shaped*; wings soar at horizontal. Likes carrion and fish.

60. COMMON CROW (*Corvus brachyrhnchos*). 17-20″. Common resident in farms, woodlands, seashores, open areas. Black all over; *tail rounded*; soars with wings bent upwards. Omnivorous, but likes corn and other grains. Loud **"caw"** cry.

61. CLARK'S NUTCRACKER (*Nucifraga columbiana*). 12-13″. Common resident in high mountain forests and alpine meadows; occasional in oak and mixed woods at lower levels in winter. *Looks like small white, gray and black crow.* Omnivorous, but especially likes pine nuts. All three of these crow-like birds can be lured by scraps of various food.

62. BLACK-CAPPED CHICKADEE (*Parus atricapillus*). (See also No.134). Resident in mountain forests from British Columbia south to northwestern California. *White sides of head contrast with black top of head*; back pale to dark gray. Many **"dee-dee"** or **"tsick-a-dee"** notes. MOUNTAIN CHICKA-DEE (*Parus gambeli*). Common resident of mountain forests. Looks like above bird, but *black head cap broken by white over eye.* Chickadees will nest in bird houses hung in trees, each with about 1¼″ hole. Loves suet, insects and bird seed (especially pine nuts).

63. PLAIN TITMOUSE (*Parus inornatus*). 5-5½″. Common resident in open woodlands, orchards and parks from southern Oregon south. *Small, gray-brown bird with crest.* **"Sick-s-dee"** call; **"sweety, sweety"** notes in song. Will nest in chickadee-size box, placed in low tree. Loves suet, insect mix, acorns and cherries.

64. COMMON BUSHTIT (*Psaltriparus minimus*). 4-4½″. Common resident in woody and brushy country except in high mountains. *Tiny, gray-backed bird with comparatively long tail.* Often flies in lightly twittering flocks. Builds beautiful hanging nest. Suet and insect mix attract, also leaf galls.

65. WRENTIT

66. DIPPER

67. HOUSE WREN

68. BEWICK'S WREN

69. LONG-BILLED MARSH WREN

70. CANYON WREN

71. ROCK WREN

Rh

WRENTIT, DIPPER AND WRENS

WRENTIT, DIPPER AND WRENS

These wrens and wren-like birds feed mainly on insects and like suet. Most wrens will take to wren-size bird houses placed in bushes or small trees.

65. WRENTIT (*Chamaea fasciata*). 6-6½″. Common resident in brush and streamside woods from coastal Oregon south. *This secretive, gray-brown bird has a long, round and cocked-up tail*; distinctive white iris. Rapid, staccato, trilling song, rising and then falling.

66. DIPPER (*Cinclus mexicanus*). 7½-8½″. Common resident by permanent streams, mainly in mountains. *Distinctive chunky body and short tail*; dark slate-gray color in spring and summer; paler gray below in fall and winter, and black bill more yellowish at base; upper eye-lid whitish. Body often dipped up and down; "flies" underwater. Clear, loud alarm note.

67. HOUSE WREN (*Troglodytes aedon*). 4½-5″. Common summer visitor in wooded, brushy and cultivated areas; also around buildings; winter visitor in California as far north as San Francisco Bay region. *Above gray-brown, with dark markings; uniform brown below*; no white marks. Scolding call notes. Often nests in buildings. WINTER WREN (*Troglodytes troglodytes*). Similar appearance, but with *very stubby tail*. Common resident in coniferous forests and streamside woods as far south as Monterey; winters in southern California. Harsh **"kt, ket"** notes.

68. BEWICK'S WREN (*Thryomanes bewickii*). 5-5½″. Common resident in brush and woods, farms and buildings, of lowlands and foothills. Brown above, white below; *white line over eye; long barred tail has narrow base and white tips on outer tail feathers*. Buzzing, gurgling and high-pitched notes.

69. LONG-BILLED MARSH WREN (*Telmatodytes palustris*). 5-6″. Lives in marshes. *Distinctive black and white striped back*; tail barred with brown; white eye stripe.

70. CANYON WREN (*Catherpes mexicanus*). 5¼-5¾″. Resident in drier areas where there are rocks and cliffs; occasionally in buildings. *Reddish-brown belly contrasts markedly with white breast and throat*; rest of body brownish. Light **"tsee"** notes.

71. ROCK WREN (*Salpinctes obsoletus*). 4½-5″. Resident in rocky country, avoiding damp coast. *White breast lightly streaked with brown*; white eye stripe. Characteristic bobbing of body. Has loud, dry, single, up-pitched trill, or a sharp **"t-keer"** note.

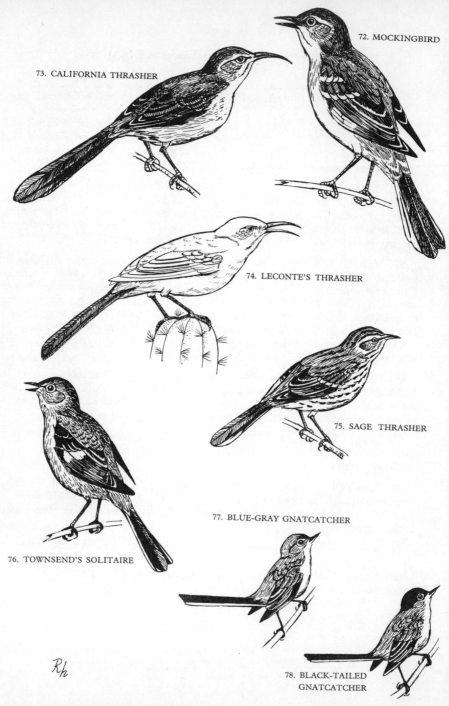

72. MOCKINGBIRD

73. CALIFORNIA THRASHER

74. LECONTE'S THRASHER

75. SAGE THRASHER

76. TOWNSEND'S SOLITAIRE

77. BLUE-GRAY GNATCATCHER

78. BLACK-TAILED GNATCATCHER

Rh

MOCKINGBIRD, THRASHERS, SOLITAIRE AND GNATCATCHERS

MOCKINGBIRD, THRASHERS, SOLITAIRE AND GNATCATCHERS

72. MOCKINGBIRD (*Mimus polyglottos*). 10-11″. Common resident of southern California and north to Sacramento and Santa Clara Valleys; in brush and gardens. *Gray above, whitish below; white patches on wings flash in flight.* Song greatly varied and often mimics other birds. Eats fruit (especially grapes, figs and berries), and insects. Robin-type nest house.

73. CALIFORNIA THRASHER (*Toxostoma redivivum*). 11-13″. Common resident in brush, streamside woods and gardens from southern California north to Shasta County. Gray brown general color; *reddish-brown under tail and on belly*; light streak over eye; *long curved bill*. Sharp **"week"** cry; long, gurgling, harsh and musical song. Eats insects, fruits and seeds. Thrashers generally nest about 4′ off ground in brush; rarely may use bird houses of robin type.

74. LECONTE'S THRASHER (*Toxostoma lecontei*). 10-11″. Resident in southern half of San Joaquin Valley and southern California in chaparral, desert scrub and farms. *Pale-colored, but has dark brown tail.*

75. SAGE THRASHER (*Oreoscoptes montanus*) 8-9″. Common winter visitor in southern San Joaquin Valley and southern California in chaparral, desert scrub and farms. *Distinguished by straight, slender bill; streaked whitish breast; 2 narrow white wing-bars on wings; white throat*; and outer tail feathers white-tipped.

76. TOWNSEND'S SOLITAIRE (*Myadestes townsendi*). 8-9½″. Common resident in high mountain forests, descending in winter to gardens and farms. *Gray above, pale gray below; white rings around eyes; wing feathers edged white*; outer tail feathers edged white. Creaky **"eesk"** call. Likes insects, seeds and berries. (Related to thrushes, numbers 138-143).

77. BLUE-GRAY GNATCATCHER (*Polioptila caerulea*). 4½-5″. Summer visitor in northern California; resident and winter visitor in south; in brush and woods. *Bluish-gray back and head; black tail with white sides*; white below. Sibilant **"spee"** note. Eats insects. Related to kinglets (see numbers 127-128).

78. BLACK-TAILED GNATCATCHER (*Polioptila melanura*). 4-4½″. Resident from Ventura County, California, south in dry brush and desert areas. *Black cap and white-edged black tail distinctive*; bluish-gray above. Has mewing and **"chee"** call. Insect-eater. (Related to kinglets numbers 127-128.)

79. HUTTON'S VIREO

80. BELL'S VIREO

81. GRAY VIREO

83. WARBLING VIREO

82. SOLITARY VIREO

84. HOUSE SPARROW ♂

85. BREWER'S BLACKBIRD ♂

86. BROWN-HEADED COWBIRD ♂

Rh

VIREOS, HOUSESPARROW, BLACKBIRDS

Vireos are small plain-colored birds, secretive and slow moving among branches. They feed on insects and nest high in branches. Small, robin-type houses might be used. (For other blackbirds see numbers 161-164.)

79. HUTTON'S VIREO (*Vireo huttoni*). 5-5½". Common resident in woods, orchards and gardens. Gray or grayish-green above, grayish-yellow below; *incomplete eye-ring broken by black spot above eye*; two white wing-bars. Hoarse, peevish note.

80. BELL'S VIREO (*Vireo bellii*). 4½-5". Common summer visitor in California valleys in streamside woods as far north as Monterey and Redding. Main difference from other vireos is that it is smaller and has a *light-grey back* Sings in soft husky whistle, usually repeated.

81. GRAY VIREO (*Vireo vicinior*). 5¼-5¾". Summer visitor in southern third of California *in brushlands*. Gray back, dull colors; *inconspicuous eye-ring*. A lively bird for a vireo. Loud, musical **"see-wee-chey-see, chee, see-chrrr-weet"** song.

82. SOLITARY VIREO (*Vireo solitarius*). 5-6". Common summer visitor in foothill and streamside woods and mountain coniferous forests. *Has bright white spectacle-like eye rings and bright white throat*; dark grayish-green above; whitish below. Very variable song, with **"chee-wee"** and **"whee-wee"** notes.

83. WARBLING VIREO (*Vireo gilvus*). 5-6". Common summer visitor in streamside and oak woods, and gardens. *Dull, grayish-brown bird with faint pale stripe above eye; no eye-ring*; whitish, yellowish-gray below. Repetitive, slow warble. May eat wild berries of dogwood, elder, snowberry and poison oak.

84. HOUSE SPARROW (*Passer domesticus*). Common resident near human dwellings. *Male with all black throat; gray on top of head; chestnut patch behind eye*. Female with grayish-brown head, brown and black streaked back. Quarrelsome **"cheep"** call. Seed eater and pest.

85. BREWER'S BLACKBIRD (*Euphagus cyanocephalus*). 8-10". See also numbers 161-163. Abundant resident in open country and woodlands. *Male black with purplish-green reflections; eye white*. Female brownish-gray. Eats insects, seeds (especially oats), and cherries. May take to robin-type house.

86. BROWN-HEADED COWBIRD (*Molothrus ater*). 8-9". Lives in California, but summer visitor farther north, in open areas and woods. *Male black with a brown head and upper neck; short, stout bill*; female brown-gray. Lays eggs in other birds' nest. Likes insects and seeds.

87. SAVANNAH SPARROW

88. VESPER SPARROW

91. SONG SPARROW

89. FOX SPARROW

90. LINCOLN'S SPARROW

93. LARK SPARROW

95. GOLDEN-CROWNE
SPARRO

96. CHIPPING SPARROW

92. GRASSHOPPER SPARROW

98. OREGON JUNCO

94. WHITE CROWNED SPARROW

RUFOUS-CROWNED
SPARROW

97. BLACK-CHINNED SPARROW

Rh

SPARROWS AND JUNCO

Sparrows are mainly seed eaters; some nest in small, robin-type houses.

87. SAVANNAH SPARROW (*Passerculus sandwichensis*). 5-6″. Resident in grasslands, marshes and seashore. *Whitish breast and sides dark brown streaked.* Soft **"tseep"** or loud **"tsup"** call notes.

88. VESPER SPARROW (*Pooecetes gramineus*). 5-6½″. Summer visitor in open dry country, from Oregon north; winter visitor from central California south. *Chestnut patch at tip of wing.* Flute-like whistle sounds like taps.

89. FOX SPARROW (*Passerella iliaca*). 6½-7½″. Summer visitor in mountain meadows; winter visitor in lowlands, in brush, streamside woods and farms. *Heavily striped breast.* Metallic **"sisp"** note.

90. LINCOLN'S SPARROW (*Melospiza lincolnii*). 5-6″. Summer visitor in mountain meadows; winter visitor from western Oregon south, in grass, marshes, farms. *Buff-colored band crosses breast*; belly finely streaked. **"Tsee"** call.

91. SONG SPARROW (*Melospiza melodia*). 5-7″. Resident in valleys and low mountains in brush, marsh, streamside woods and gardens. *Dark streaks on breast merge into large spot.* **"Tchik"** call note; melodious song starts with **"seet-seet-sweet"** notes.

92. GRASSHOPPER SPARROW (*Ammodramus savannarum*). 4-5″. Summer visitor in grasslands, farms; winter visitor in central California and south. *Dark back striped with reddish-brown.* Dry trill or buzzing song; light **"tlick"** note.

93. LARK SPARROW (*Chondestes grammacus*). 5½-6½″. Summer visitor in Oregon; resident in California in grass, brush and oaks. *White and dark-marked face distinctive.* Soft **"tseep"** call note; buzzing, churring, trilling song.

94. WHITE CROWNED SPARROW (*Zonotrichia leucophrys*). 6-7″. Common resident in brush and grassy hills and streamside woods; summer visitor in mountain meadows. *Black and white head; gray breast.* Metallic **"pink"** note.

95. GOLDEN-CROWNED SPARROW (*Zonotrichia atricapilla*). 6-7″. Winter visitor in brush, streamside woods, coastal forest, grass and gardens. *Yellow or yellow-orange crown.* 3-noted song, coming down in scale like "3 Blind Mice."

96. CHIPPING SPARROW (*Spizella passerina*). 5-5½″. Summer visitor in mountain meadows, coastal forests, woodlands, gardens. *Reddish-brown crown; dark eye line; notched tail.* Light **"sip"** call. RUFOUS-CROWNED SPARROW (*Aimophila ruficeps*). Similar, but *black mark on side of throat and tail rounded.* Resident in California brush and grass. Musical **"dreer"** note.

97. BLACK-CHINNED SPARROW (*Spizella atrogularis*). 5″. Central California and south in brush. *Distinctive black chin and throat.* Faint **"tchip"** call.

98. OREGON JUNCO (*Junco oreganus*). 5-6″. Resident in woods, forests, and gardens. *Black head; reddish-brown back.* Makes twittering and clicking notes; loud, buzzing song.

103. MOURNING DOVE

99. BAND-TAILED PIGEON

101. SPOTTED DOVE

102. RINGED TURTLE DOVE

100. ROCK DOVE

Rosinda Holmes

PIGEONS, DOVES

104. BLACK-CHINNED HUMMINGBIRD

105. COSTA'S HUMMINGBIRD

106. ANNA'S HUMMINGBIRD

107. RUFOUS HUMMINGBIRD

108. ALLEN'S HUMMINGBIRD

109. CALLIOPE HUMMINGBIRD

HUMMINGBIRDS

PIGEONS, DOVES AND HUMMINGBIRDS

Pigeons and doves live mainly on seeds, waste grain, fruits and insects. Some can be induced to nest in platforms put in bushes or low trees, but the rock dove (domestic pigeon) will nest best in large size robin-like bird house on building ledge.

99. BAND-TAILED PIGEON (*Columba fasciata*). 14-16". Summer visitor, mainly in mountain and coastal coniferous forests; winter visitor and sometimes resident in lower hilly country oaks, farms and gardens. *Bluish-gray above with black-tipped wings; broad gray band across end of wide tail and white neck crescent distinctive.* Strange, owl-like **"whoo-oo-oo"** call. Likes acorns, cherries, oats, wheat.

100. ROCK DOVE or DOMESTIC PIGEON (*Columba livia*). 14-16". Resident here and there near towns and in rocky canyons, in grass, brush, farms, gardens and parks. *Head, neck and body purplish-gray, somewhat iridescent.* Soft, cooing call.

101. SPOTTED DOVE (*Streptopelia chinensis*). 13-14". Introduced resident in Los Angeles area and north to Santa Barbara, in farms, gardens and streamside woods. *White spots on black sides and back of neck*; white corners to tail. **"Coo-whoo-coo-coo"** call.

102. RINGED TURTLE DOVE (*Streptopelia risoria*). 11-13". Introduced around Los Angeles, in gardens, buildings, streamside woods. *Narrow black ring encircles back and sides of neck*; pale brown general color. Purring **"coo"** call.

103. MOURNING DOVE (*Zenaidura macroura*). 11-13". Summer visitor from British Columbia to Oregon; resident in California; in woodlands, grass, brush, farms and gardens. *Central brown tail feathers; outer tail feathers gray, tipped with white, bordered with black*; pinkish-brown breast; reddish-brown on head. **"Coo-coo-coo"** call.

Hummingbirds can be lured by hummingbird feeders with sweetened water. Hummingbird females and young are often almost impossible to tell apart.

104. BLACK-CHINNED HUMMINGBIRD (*Archilochus alexandri*). 3½-4". Common summer visitor in streamside woods, oaks and mountain forests in California north to Shasta County. *White band beneath black chin and throat of male, which appear purple in certain lights.* Male whirrs back and forth in small arc when courting.

HUMMINGBIRDS AND WOODPECKERS

105. COSTA'S HUMMINGBIRD (*Calypte costae*). 2¾-3¼″. Common summer visitor in southern California brush, farms and gardens. *Male's forehead and throat violet-purple; throat feathers conspicuous.* Female of this and Black-chinned Hummingbird paler than other female hummers with no rufous or red in markings. Male makes U-shaped courting dive and hiss.

106. ANNA'S HUMMINGBIRD (*Calypte anna*). 3½-4″. Common resident in most of low elevation California outside of deserts and coniferous forests, in brush, hardwoods, eucalyptus, and gardens; visits northwestern California forests in fall. *Male with bright rosy-red forehead and throat. Rose-red mark on female's throat.* Male makes V-shaped mating arc and squeaky buzz.

107. RUFOUS HUMMINGBIRD (*Selasphorus rufus*). 3¼-4″. Common summer visitor from mountains of northwest California to Alaska, in forest edges and wooded gardens; spring migrant through California, in brush, hardwoods and gardens; late summer migrant in forests or mountains. *Male with bright coppery-red throat; both sexes with bright reddish-brown upper parts.* Male makes tight circle at oblique angle in mating arc, with ripping sound.

108. ALLEN'S HUMMINGBIRD (*Selasphorus sasin*). 3-3¼″. Common summer visitor along California coast. *Brilliant orange-red or red throat in male; reddish-brown rump in both sexes.* Male makes U-shaped mating arc.

109. CALLIOPE HUMMINGBIRD (*Stellula calliope*). 3½-4″. Common summer visitor in mountain forests, meadows and brush. *Brilliant lilac feathers appear lance-like against white background on throat of male*; head and back golden-green. *Female bronzy-green above, with speckled white throat.* Male makes narrow U-shaped dive.

Most woodpeckers eat grubs they dig out of bark and wood of trees. A few will use sparrow-hawk type houses if shaped like a stump.

110. RED-SHAFTED FLICKER (*Colaptes cafer*). 12-14″. Resident in hardwoods, coniferous forests, farms, buildings, and gardens. *Red under wing and tail*; black crescent on breast; *male with red marks on cheeks.* Head often bobs energetically. Many loud cries. Likes ants, grapes, apples, acorns and corn especially.

110. RED-SHAFTED FLICKER

♀

♀

♂

111. YELLOW-SHAFTED FLICKER

♂

113. PILEATED WOODPECKER

112. LEWIS' WOODPECKER

122. NUTTALL'S WOODPECKER

121. DOWNY
WOODPECKER

119. WHITE-HEADED
WOODPECKER

120. HAIRY WOODPECKER

Rosinda
Holmes

WOODPECKERS

111. YELLOW-SHAFTED FLICKER (*Colaptes auratus*). 12-14″. Summer visitor to central British Columbia; rare transient elsewhere; in grasslands, buildings, gardens, farms. Similar to Red-shafted Flicker except has yellow wing and tail linings and *red crescent-shaped mark on back of head*; also *mark under cheek of male is black.*

112. LEWIS' WOODPECKER (*Asyndesmus lewis*). 10½-11½″. Resident in mountain forests, oaks and wooded gardens, but comes down from high altitudes and north in winter to some extent. *Rose-red belly and cheeks, plus dark color, are distinctive.* Especially likes acorns, elderberries, apples, pine nuts and cherries.

113. PILEATED WOODPECKER (*Dryocopus pileatus*). 17-18″. Resident in thick coniferous forests from central Sierras and Sonoma County north. *Large, crow-sized, black woodpecker with top of head forming flaming red and pointed crest*; narrow white line above eye; *white zig-zag mark on neck.* Very loud **"kek-kek-kek"** cry.

114. BLACK-BACKED THREE-TOED WOODPECKER (*Picoides arcticus*). 9-10″. Resident in sub-alpine forests of high Sierra; rarely comes lower down. *Male has yellow cap* (lacking in female); *rest of upper parts black except for white marks on face and tail;* white below. Tears bark.

115. NORTHERN THREE-TOED WOODPECKER (*Picoides tridactylus*). 9-10″. Resident in high mountain forests from Oregon north. Similar to above bird, but with *white ladder on back.* Most woodpeckers have two toes forward and two back, but these two species have only one toe pointing back. Both have sharp **"kick"** call notes.

116. RED-BREASTED SAPSUCKER (*Sphyrapicus varius*). 8-9″. Common summer visitor in northern coniferous forests and in high mountains of California; winter visitor to oak and streamside woods, farms and gardens of lowlands. *Breast, neck and head bright crimson red*; white spots on black wings and back; white middle of tail and on rump, and white band along bend of wing. Immature bird duller with mottled gray. Forms holes on tree in girdling circle. A nasal **"chrrr"** cry and squeal. Likes berries, grapes, and apples especially; also sucks sap from trees.

WOODPECKERS

117. WILLIAMSON'S SAPSUCKER (*Sphyrapicus thyroideus*). 9-10″. Common summer visitor in mountain coniferous forests; winters in woods and wooded gardens of lowlands. Upper parts of male all black except for white stripes below and behind eye, and white patch at bend of wing; white rump; yellow belly; red chin. Female much lighter colored and ladder-backed. Nasal **"weee-er"** cry. Drinks tree sap; particularly likes ants and beetles.

118. ACORN WOODPECKER (*Melanerpes formicivorus*). 9-10″. Resident in oak woods, coniferous forests, farms, buildings and gardens from Oregon south. *Red on top of head; yellow throat*; white on forehead; black around eye; white wing patches show in flight; female with black on forehead. Stores acorns in holes in dead stumps, etc. **"Wick-up"** or **"jay-cup"** calls. Especially likes acorns, corn, almonds and walnuts, also ants.

119. WHITE-HEADED WOODPECKER 9-10″ (*Dendrocopos albolarvatus*). 8½-9″. Common resident of mountain coniferous forests. The only one of our woodpeckers with *white head and throat*; red on nape of neck; black on rest of body except for white on wings. Gives shrill **"wick-wick"** or sharp, rattling cry. Particularly likes pinyon pine nuts and ants.

120. HAIRY WOODPECKER (*Dendrocopos villosus*). 9-10″. Resident in coniferous forests, streamside woods, and sometimes wooded gardens. *Has distinctive white and black color design plus large size.* Loud **"kink"** note and rattle.

121. DOWNY WOODPECKER (*Dendrocopos pubescens*). 6½-7″. Resident principally in streamside woods, also oaks, open coastal coniferous forests, farms and gardens. Looks just like the Hairy Woodpecker except for *small size, slender bill, and inconspicuous black bars on outer tail feathers.* Particularly likes dog woodberries, corn, acorns and apples.

122. NUTTALL'S WOODPECKER (*Dendrocopos nuttallii*). 7″. Resident in California from Redding and southern Humboldt County south in oak and streamside woods, farms and gardens. *White cross stripes or "ladder" on black back are very distinctive*; red on back of head; underparts are white with black spots on sides. Sharp **"prrrt"** and buzzing calls. Likes berries.

115. NORTHERN THREE-
TOED WOODPECKER

114. BLACK-BACKED THREE-
TOED WOODPECKER

116. RED-BREASTED
SAPSUCKER

118. ACORN WOODPECKER

117. WILLIAMSON'S SAPSUCKER

125. WESTERN KINGBIRD

126. CASSIN'S KINGBIRD

♂

♀

123. VERMILION FLYCATCHER

♀

127. RUBY-CROWNED KINGLET

♂

128. GOLDEN-CROWNED KINGLET

♀

♂

Rosinca Holmes

FLYCATCHERS AND KINGLETS

FLYCATCHERS AND KINGLETS

The first four birds illustrated on page 43 are members of the flycatcher family. Flycatchers fly out from a branch to catch an insect and then fly back. Other flycatchers are numbered 44-49. Kingbirds will often take to robin-type bird-houses if these are placed from 10-35' above ground with good view. The kinglets and related gnatcatchers (numbers 77-78) feed on small insects and suet hung high in trees.

123. VERMILION FLYCATCHER (*Pyrocephalus rubinus*). 5½-6½". Fall visitor to southern California coast in streamside woods. *Male with bright scarlet under parts and head* (which may show crest); black line through eye. Female and young are mainly brown above except for black tail. Sharp **"pssk"** and weak **"pet-a-see"** notes.

124. TROPICAL KINGBIRD (*Tyrannus melancholicus*). 8-9½". *Fall visitor to southern California in streamside woods. The forked, dusky-brown tail without white edgings* marks it differently from other kingbirds. Nasal **"keer"** or **"chee-keer"** notes.

125. WESTERN KINGBIRD (*Tyrannus verticalis*). 8-9". Common summer visitor, mainly in grassy areas, farms and gardens of interior valleys and hills. *Black tail bordered with white*; pale gray head, back and chest; wings brownish; body yellowish below. Gives shrill peevish cries and often attacks other birds. Likes elderberries.

126. CASSIN'S KINGBIRD (*Tyrannus vociferans*). 8½-9". Resident chiefly in coast range valleys south from San Benito County, California. Similar to Western Kingbird, but *black tail without white sides*; dark gray back. Harsh low call. Likes grapes, elderberries and olives.

127. RUBY-CROWNED KINGLET (*Regulus calendula*). 4-4½". Summer visitor in high mountain forests; winters in hardwoods, coastal fir forest, farms and gardens in lower country. Olive-gray above; *bright white eye-ring*; male rarely shows red crown patch. Likes small galls and elderberries; insects.

128. GOLDEN-CROWNED KINGLET (*Regulus satrapa*). 3½-4". Resident in high mountains and humid coastal forest; winter visitor along central Californian coast and less commonly to south. *Has bright orange crown bordered by black and yellow.* Has weak **"see-see-see"** notes.

129. LOGGERHEAD SHRIKE (*Lanius ludovicianus*). 8-10″. Resident in California grasslands, sage and oak woods. *Typical black, gray and white design*; differs from Northern Shrike by *black lines through eyes joining over bill*, also by lack of markings on belly. All shrikes tear flesh of animals with hooked bill or impale lizards, mice, birds, etc. on barbed wire or thorns; they will also eat hamburger. Flies with quick, sharp wing beats, then makes sudden upward glide to perch. Harsh **"tree"** cry. May take to robin-type bird house in large bush or small tree.

130. NORTHERN SHRIKE (*Lanius excubitor*). 7½-8½″. Irregular winter visitor in open grassland, farms or brush south to Oregon. Looks almost exactly like Loggerhead Shrike except for stronger, more sharply hooked bill, faintly barred breast, and the *black bar broken in front of eye*; young bird brown in color. Has harsh **"tree"** cry; also **"tree-lip"** or **"chee-rrr."**

Jays feed on almost anything and are easily attracted by food scraps, suet, bird seed, etc. Robin-type houses hidden in appropriate conifers for Gray and Steller's Jays, or in bushes for Scrub Jay may attract them.

131. STELLER'S JAY (*Cyanocitta stelleri*). 12-13½″. Common resident in hardwood and coniferous forests, rare in gardens. *Upper back, chest and head dark brownish-black*, rest of body deep blue; *only jay with crest*. Many harsh notes, including very rapid **"chey-chey-chey-chey"** call; often mimics shrill scream of Red-tailed Hawk.

132. SCRUB JAY (*Aphelocoma coerulescens*). 11-12″. Common resident from southwestern Washington south in hardwoods, brush, farms and gardens. *Upper parts blue except for brown back; belly and throat light gray except for dark band across breast*. Harsh **"chey-chey-chey"** cry, but slower and shriller than Steller's Jay.

133. GRAY JAY (*Perisoreus canadensis*). 11-12″. Common resident in Mendocino County, California north in coniferous forests. *Black above except for white on top of head*; lower neck with grayish-white collar. Harsh, screaming calls of **"ker-wheep!"**

129. LOGGERHEAD SHRIKE

131. STELLER'S JAY

132. SCRUB JAY

133. GRAY JAY

Rosinta Holmes

SHRIKES AND JAYS

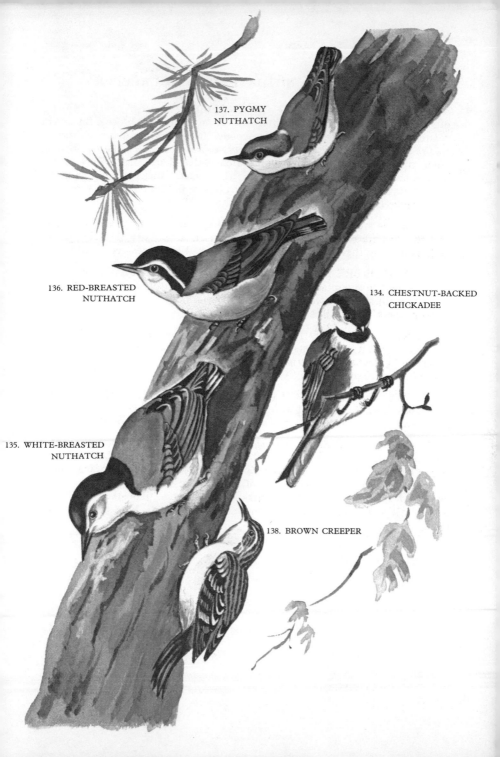

137. PYGMY
NUTHATCH

136. RED-BREASTED
NUTHATCH

134. CHESTNUT-BACKED
CHICKADEE

135. WHITE-BREASTED
NUTHATCH

138. BROWN CREEPER

CHICKADEES, NUTHATCHES AND CREEPER

CHICKADEES, NUTHATCHES AND CREEPER

134. CHESTNUT-BACKED CHICKADEE (*Parus rufescens*). (See also number 62.) 4½-5″. Resident from Alaska to central California in coastal coniferous forest, oaks, streamside woods, farms and gardens. *Distinctive reddish-brown back, dark cap, black throat, white cheeks.* Very active in trees, often upside down. Rasping **"sick-sick-a-dee-dee!"** call. Eats mainly insects, also pine nuts, berries and seeds; likes suet. Chickadees like to nest in warm sunny places not more than 10′ high; best to put up chickadee-type house with disguised nest hole.

Nuthatches are mainly feeders on small insects, but they also eat seeds, particularly seeds of pine and fir; all like suet. Since they usually build nests in hollows in trees, they will often occupy log-shaped chickadee-type bird houses.

135. WHITE-BREASTED NUTHATCH (*Sitta carolinensis*). 5-6″. Common resident in mountain coniferous forests, oak woods, farms and gardens. *Distinctive white breast, bluish-gray back and black cap and back of neck.* Nasal **"kyeer-kyeer"** call. Likes acorns and wheat.

136. RED-BREASTED NUTHATCH (*Sitta canadensis*). 4-6″. Common resident of coniferous forests, especially fir; occasional winter visitor in oak woods and gardens. *Black stripe through eye, white line above eye and black top of head are distinctive.* Nasal **"yhank-yhank"** call; also shrill **"ket-ket-ket."**

137. PYGMY NUTHATCH (*Sitta pygmaea*). 4-4½″. Common resident of coniferous forests; occasional winter visitor in gardens. Gray-brown cap comes down over eye; white throat; gray belly. Shrill, staccato **"tee-dee"** call.

138. BROWN CREEPER (*Certhia familiaris*). 5-5½″. Common resident of thick coniferous forests and oak woodlands; rare in gardens. *Slender, downward-curved bill; whitish streaks on brown above. Tail used as prop in climbing;* climbs in upward spiral, then flies to base of nearby tree to start again, continually hunting for insects in cracks of bark. Soft, lisping **"tsee-tsee-tsee"** call. Rarely will nest in chickadee bird house. Besides insects, likes pine nuts and corn.

THRUSHES

Birds on this page are of the Thrush Family. Most are fine singers. They feed on worms, snails, insects, seeds, berries and other fruit, and will come to suet. Bluebirds will nest in bluebird-type bird houses; others usually like robin-type open houses. (See also number 76.)

139. WESTERN BLUEBIRD (*Sialia mexicana*). 6-7". Common summer visitor in open coniferous forests and foothill woodlands; winter visitor from Puget Sound south in gardens, farms, grasslands and woodlands. *Male has mainly dark blue upper parts, and blue throat; breast and upper back reddish.* Female brownish and reddish-brown. Rapidly repeated **"puw-puw"** call. Especially likes grapes, mistletoe berries and elderberries.

140. MOUNTAIN BLUEBIRD (*Sialia currocoides*). 6½-8". Irregular winter visitor in open woods and grasslands, uncommon in gardens and farms; uncommon summer visitor on the crest of the Sierras and Cascades. *Male pale azure blue over most of body;* female brownish with blue on tail region and wings. Often hovers. Likes grapes.

141. ROBIN (*Turdus migratorius*). 9-11". Common summer visitor in coniferous forests, streamside woods, grass, farms, gardens, oaks; winters from Washington south at lower elevations. *Male in spring and summer has rusty-red breast and gray back;* female has grayish head and tail; breast pale reddish-brown. Both sexes in winter are browner, while the reddish breast is obscured by white markings. Cheerful, rising and falling, four note song. Especially likes peppertree, berries, grapes, prunes and cherries.

142. VARIED THRUSH (*Ixoreus naevius*). 9-10". Summer visitor in coastal coniferous forests from Mendocino County, California, north. Common winter visitor in brush, farms and gardens. Looks like a robin, but has *black band* across reddish-brown breast. Female has gray breast band. Soft **"tchook"** call. Likes acorns, berries, apples and prunes.

143. SWAINSON'S THRUSH (*Hylocichla ustulata*). 6½-8". Common summer visitor in coastal coniferous forests, streamside woods, farms, gardens, especially near water. *All olive or gray-brown above; yellowish-brown eye ring.* Soft, beautiful, upward-spiralling song. Likes cherries and berries.

144. HERMIT THRUSH (*Hylocichla guttata*). 6½-8". Summer visitor in high mountains and coastal coniferous forests; common winter visitor in streamside woods, farms, marshes, gardens of lower elevations. *Reddish-brown tail and rump.* Exquisitely lovely, flute-like song. Likes peppertree and poison oak berries.

139. WESTERN BLUEBIRD

140. MOUNTAIN BLUEBIRD

♂

♀

♂

♀

141. ROBIN

142. VARIED THRUSH

♀

♂

143. SWAINSON'S THRUSH

144. HERMIT THRUSH

Rosinda Holmes

THRUSHES

145. CEDAR WAXWING

146. BOHEMIAN WAXWING

47. PHAINOPEPLA ♂

♀

148. STARLING

Adult in winter

Adult in spring

WAXWINGS, PHAINOPEPLA, STARLING AND WARBLERS

WAXWINGS, PHAINOPEPLA, STARLING AND WARBLERS

145. CEDAR WAXWING (*Bombycilla cedrorum*). 6½-8". Resident as far south as northwestern California, in open coastal coniferous forests and streamside woods; wide-spread winter visitor in orchards and gardens. A handsome, *crested brown bird, with waxy red spots on each wing; yellow band across end of tail.* High-pitched whistle. Especially likes insects, peppertree berries, grapes and cherries; try suet. Use robin-type house.

146. BOHEMIAN WAXWING (*Bombycilla garrula*). 7½-9". Summer visitor to British Columbia and northern Washington, in coniferous forests and marsh; sporadic winter visitor as far south as central California in woods. Similar to above, but with *white spots on wings.*

147. PHAINOPEPLA (*Phainopepla nitens*). 7-8". Summer visitor north to Shasta County, California in oak woods, farms and gardens of dry valleys. *Male glossy black with slender crest; bright white wing patches*; female uniform gray. An expert flycatcher. Wheezy, soft and broken song. Likes insects, elderberries, other berries, grapes and cherries.

148. STARLING (*Sturnus vulgaris*). 7½-8½". Flocks are resident in many towns, grasslands, farms, gardens; mainly migratory in Washington and British Columbia. *Long yellow bill is distinctive; also glossy purple and green tints on black plumage in spring*; in winter the black is speckled with white; immature is blackish-gray. Omnivorous pest.

Warblers are usually smaller than sparrows and brightly-colored (usually with some yellow), actively flitting birds. Most live on insects and come to suet. A few will come to nest in chickadee-type bird houses.

149. ORANGE-CROWNED WARBLER (*Vermivora celata*). 4-5". Common migrant and summer visitor at low and middle elevations in brush, hardwoods, coniferous forests, farms and gardens. Plain-looking warbler, olive-green above, yellowish-green below. Weak, repeated trill for song; soft **"chip"** call.

WARBLERS

150. NASHVILLE WARBLER (*Vermivora ruficapilla*). 4-5″. Common summer visitor in mountain forests, oak and brush covered hills, south to central California; migrant in southern California. *Male with bright yellow belly; distinct white eye-ring*; ashy-gray top and sides of head. Female duller. Shrill **"see-lit"** song.

151. YELLOW WARBLER (*Dendroica petechia*). 4-5″. Common migrant and summer visitor in hardwoods, farms, gardens, always near water. *Only all yellow warbler*, but streaked reddish-brown below. Soft **"see-see-weetee-see"** song; soft **"tsick"** call.

152. MYRTLE WARBLER (*Dendroica coronata*). 5-6″. Common winter visitor from Oregon south in hardwoods, coniferous forests (at low or medium elevations), farms and gardens. *Throat white and 2-3 outer tail feathers on each side flash white spots*. Otherwise similar to number 153. Soft, but harsh **"tsip"** call. Likes figs.

153. AUDUBON'S WARBLER (*Dendroica auduboni*). 4¾-5½″. Common summer visitor in mountain forests; common migrant and winter visitor in coastal coniferous forest, grasslands, hardwoods, farms and gardens. *Both sexes show bright yellow rumps and yellow patches on sides of breast*; white wing patches appear in spring; in winter both become brownish above; male shows yellow crown in spring. Particularly likes figs.

154. BLACK-THROATED GRAY WARBLER (*Dendroica nigrescens*). 4½-5″. Summer visitor in foothill oaks, and open coniferous forests; winters from southern California south in oaks and gardens. *Male gray with black and white designed head*; female has whitish throat. Variable, wheezy song.

155. HERMIT WARBLER (*Dendroica occidentalis*). 4½-5″. Summer visitor to British Columbia and Washington in coniferous forests; in mountain coniferous forests to south; widespread migrant and rare winter visitor in hardwoods and gardens. *Male with yellow head, black throat*. **"Tssk"** call.

156. TOWNSEND'S WARBLER (*Dendroica townsendi*). 4½-5″. Summer visitor in coniferous forests of British Columbia and Washington; winter visitor in oak woods and gardens elsewhere. *Male in spring and summer with black crown; green and yellow around eye*. Female (and male in winter) has greenish head, yellowish-black throat. Variable, wheezy song, starting with **"tzeedle-tzeedle."**

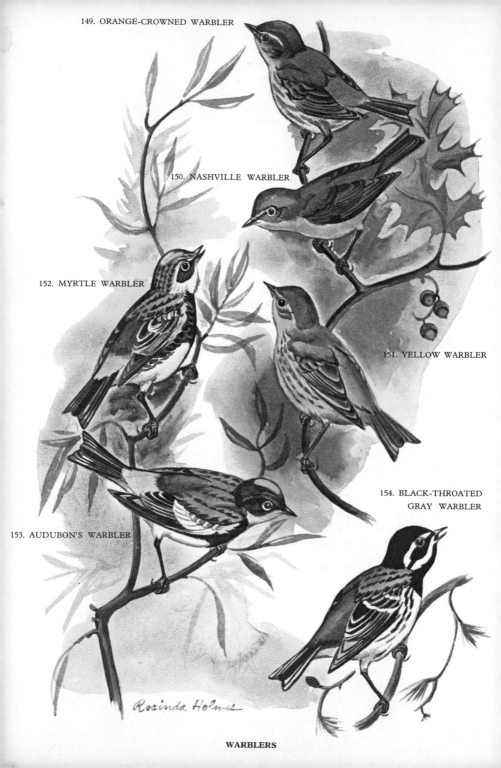

149. ORANGE-CROWNED WARBLER

150. NASHVILLE WARBLER

152. MYRTLE WARBLER

151. YELLOW WARBLER

154. BLACK-THROATED
GRAY WARBLER

153. AUDUBON'S WARBLER

Rosinda Holmes

WARBLERS

156. TOWNSEND'S WARBLER
♂
♀

155. HERMIT WARBLER
♂
♀

157. MACGILLIVRAY'S WARBLER
♀
♂

158. YELLOWTHROAT
♂

♂

159. YELLOW-BREASTED CHAT

♀

160. WILSON'S (*Pileolated*) WARBLER

157. MACGILLIVRAY'S WARBLER (*Oporornis tolmiei*). 4¾-5½″. Common summer visitor in Sierras and Coast Range from San Francisco Bay area north in coniferous forests, brush, streamside woods, oaks and wooded gardens; widespread migrant. *Male with dark gray hood, white eye-ring*; female has paler hood. **"Tsskk"** call, or **"peet"** note.

158. YELLOWTHROAT (*Geothlypis trichas*). 4½-5¾″. Common widespread migrant; common resident in fresh-water marshes in southern California; summer visitor from central California north in marshes and streamside woods. *Yellow throat and black mask in male*; female mostly dull olive-brown above, but has yellow throat. Scolding voice.

159. YELLOW-BREASTED CHAT (*Icteria virens*). 6½-7½″. Widely distributed, common summer visitor near lakes and streams in streamside woods and brush, sometimes in gardens; migrant along streams; absent in high mountains. *Very large, yellow-breasted warbler with bright white spectacle-like eye-rings*. Loud, odd, harsh, whistled song. Likes berries.

160. WILSON'S (*Pileolated*) WARBLER (*Wilsonia pulsilla*). 4-5″. Common migrant and summer visitor near lakes and streams in streamside woods, oaks, brush, coastal coniferous forest and sub-alpine forests. *Bright yellow beneath*; olive-green above; *black eye on yellow face; male has black cap*. Rapid **"chit-chit-chit"** song, getting loud and fast.

Meadowlarks, blackbirds and orioles feed on insects, fruit and seeds. (See also blackbirds numbers 85 and 86.)

161. WESTERN MEADOWLARK (*Sturnella neglecta*). 8-10″. Widespread, abundant resident in grasslands, marshes and farms. Male has whitesided tail, *bright yellow breast with black* **V**. Female duller. Cheerful, bubbling song; **"tchuk"** call. Nests in grass. Likes oats and wheat.

162. REDWINGED BLACKBIRD (*Agelaius phoeniceus*). 7-9½″. Resident, generally near standing water in marshes, grasslands and farms; rare at higher elevations. Male entirely black with red and yellow patch on wing. Metallic, gurgling song. Likes oats, wheat, barley and corn.

163. TRICOLORED BLACKBIRD (*Agelaius tricolor*). 7-9″. *Male has 3-color wing patch*; otherwise same as above bird.

BLACKBIRDS, ORIOLES, TANAGER, FINCHES

164. YELLOW-HEADED BLACKBIRD (*Xanthocephalus xanthocephalus*). 8-10½″. Common summer visitor in marshes and farms (near water); common migrant except in humid coast forest; winters sparingly in southern California. *Male black except for bright yellow head, neck and chest,* and white wing patch. Raspy, creaky song. Likes bristlegrass, oats, and corn.

165. BULLOCK'S ORIOLE (*Icterus bullockii*). 7-8½″. Common summer visitor near streams in open woods; migrant also in grasslands, farms and gardens. *Male with black top of head, upper back and throat; black line through eye; orange body.* Female more yellowish-gray. Sharp **"skit"** call. May nest in hanging gourd with 2½″ hole. Likes fruits, especially cherries, figs and raspberries.

166. HOODED ORIOLE (*Icterus cucullatus*). 7-8″. Summer visitor in streamside woods, savannah, farms and gardens, in lowlands of south half of California. *Male with black throat, tail, wings and middle back;* white wing bars; *rest orange.* Scolding **"krrrk!"** cry. Orioles may be attracted to suet or insect mixes hung in net bags in trees. Likes figs.

167. WESTERN TANAGER (*Piranga ludoviciana*). 6-7″. Common migrant in wooded areas and wooded gardens; common summer visitor in open coniferous forests of mountains. *Bright red head and yellow and black body of male;* female duller. **"Peer-ee, peer-ee"** phrases in song. Likes cherries, berries and insects, also suet.

Family of Finches on following pages are all mainly seed eaters with stout bills, but some like fruit. Most eat bird seed, suet and insect mix. A few, which nest in trees or bushes, may be attracted by robin-type bird houses, fitted to size.

168. CARDINAL (*Richmondena cardinalis*). 8-9″. Introduced resident in southern California streamside woods, farms and gardens. The only bright red male bird with a crest; female paler. Likes grapes, corn and berries.

169. BLACK-HEADED GROSBEAK (*Pheucticus melanocephalus*). 6½-8″. Common summer visitor in streamside woods, oaks, coniferous forests, farms and gardens. *Male with black head, reddish-brown neck and breast,* yellow belly; female duller. Likes figs, cherries, berries and insects.

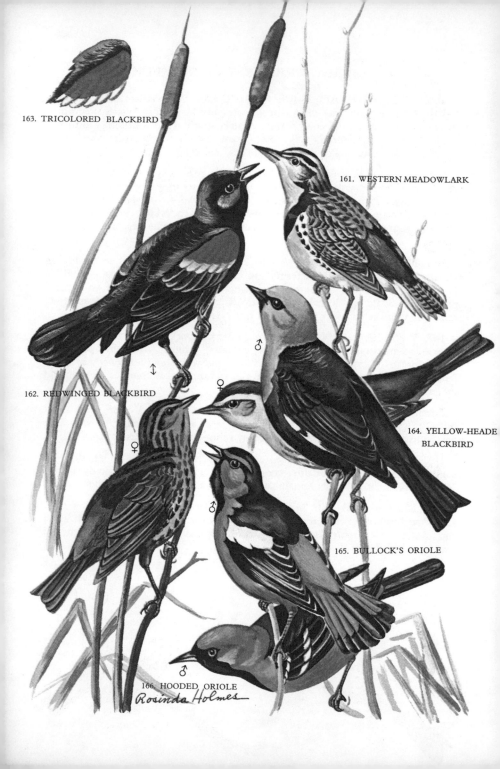

163. TRICOLORED BLACKBIRD

161. WESTERN MEADOWLARK

♂

162. REDWINGED BLACKBIRD

♀

♀

164. YELLOW-HEADE
BLACKBIRD

♂

165. BULLOCK'S ORIOLE

♂

166. HOODED ORIOLE

Rosinda Holmes

167. WESTERN TANAGER

168. CARDINAL

169. BLACK-HEADED GROSBEAK

170. BLUE GROSBEAK

171. PINE GROSBEAK

172. EVENING GROSBEAK

GROSBEAKS, PURPLE FINCHES AND BUNTING

170. BLUE GROSBEAK (*Guiraca caerulea*). 6½-8". Common summer visitor in central valley and coastal southern California in streamside woods, marshes, farms, gardens and brush. *Male dark blue with two reddish-brown wing bars*; female has yellow-brown wing bars, light brown body. **"Peeenk"** note. Likes bristlegrass, wheat and corn.

171. PINE GROSBEAK (*Pinicola enucleator*). 7½-9½". Resident in high mountain coniferous forests south to central Sierra. *Male red on head, back and breast*; black wings with white bars (actually more a purple finch type); female browner. Especially likes snowberries, willow seeds and dogwood berries.

172. EVENING GROSBEAK (*Hesperiphona vespertina*). 7-8½". Resident or summer visitor in coniferous forests; may winter in foothill woods and wooded gardens. *Male with top of head black; also wings and tail; yellow forehead and over-eye line; large white patch on wing*; female duller. **"Tseeer-ee"** call. Likes table scraps, pine and cedar nuts, cherries and berries.

173. PURPLE FINCH (*Carpodacus purpureus*). 5½-6½". Common resident in mountain and coastal coniferous forests; winter visitor to oak and streamside woods in lowlands, also farms and gardens. *Male brown with rose-red on head, breast and rump*; whitish below, but without dark streakings on under parts like similar house finch; *tip of tail notched*. All *Carpodacus* females are streaked gray-brown. Metallic **"pick"** note. Likes many buds and fruits.

174. CASSIN'S FINCH (*Carpodacus cassinii*. 6-6½". Common resident in mountain forests. Similar to purple finch, but larger and male paler red on breast; *square red patch on crown sharply contrasts with brown neck and back*; *tail deeply notched*. Startling **"tay-dee-yeep"** note.

175. HOUSE FINCH (*Carpodacus mexicanus*). 5-6". Abundant resident in open country, town, gardens, woods, brush. Similar to above finches, but *male brown with bright red rump, forehead, breast and eye stripe*. May use large wren-size house. Likes many seeds, also figs and prunes.

176. LAZULI BUNTING (*Passerina amoena*). 5-5½". Common summer visitor and migrant in brush, grasslands, streamside and oak woods, farms and gardens in lower country. Male bright blue on upper parts; female dull brown. **"Tskik"** alarm note. Likes oats, miners lettuce, seeds and insects.

CROSSBILLS, SISKIN, GOLDFINCHES AND TOWHEES

177. RED CROSSBILL (*Loxia curvirostra*). 5-6½". Common resident in coniferous forests; winter visitor irregularly to lower country in streamside woods and gardens. *Distinctive bill with crossed tips; male dull red* (or rarely yellow green to orange) all over; female duller. Likes nuts of pines and other conifers.

178. PINE SISKIN (*Spinus pinus*). 4½-5". Common resident in coniferous forests and cool woodlands; winter visitor irregularly in brush, farms and gardens. Streaked dusky to yellowish-brown; yellow blotch in wing. Talkative twitter. Especially likes filaree seeds and pine nuts.

179. AMERICAN GOLDFINCH (*Spinus tristis*). 4½-5½". Common resident in low country in streamside woods, brush, grass, farms and gardens. *Male bright yellow with black wings with white bars, black tail and forehead* (summer). Male duller and like female in winter. Sweet, twittering call. Especially likes sunflower, filaree and star thistle seeds.

180. LESSER GOLDFINCH (*Spinus psaltria*). 3¾-4". Abundant resident or summer visitor from Oregon south in open areas, woods, brush, coastal coniferous forest, farms and gardens. *Male with greenish-black back, black cap, yellow below*. Plaintive **"tee-yeer"** notes. Likes star thistle and other weed seeds.

181. LAWRENCE'S GOLDFINCH (*Spinus lawrencei*). 4-4½". Summer visitor from central California south; winter visitor in southern California, in woods, conifers, grass, brush, gardens. *Male with gray head, black face and chin*; yellow throat, breast, rump and wing bars; female lacks black areas. Sharp **"trik"** note. Likes weed seeds.

182. GREEN-TAILED TOWHEE (*Chlorura chlorura*). 6½-7". Common summer visitor to brush of high mountains; winter visitor in southern California. *Sparrow-like bird with bright white throat and reddish-brown crown; greenish above*. **"Mew"** call. Likes insects, seeds, berries and miners lettuce.

183. RUFOUS-SIDED TOWHEE (*Pipilo erythrophthalmus*). 7-8½". Common resident of brush, woods, coastal forest, farms, gardens. Distinctive *white-spotted wings, reddish-brown sides and black back*. **"Meow"**-like call. Likes acorns, raspberries and various weed seeds; also insects.

184. BROWN TOWHEE (*Pipilo fuscus*). 8-9". Common resident from southwest Oregon south in brush, woods, coastal coniferous forests, farms and gardens. *Brown; generally reddish-brown under tail*. Quarrelsome, buzzy notes. Likes oats, barley, rye grass and various seeds.

173. PURPLE FINCH ♀ ♂

174. CASSIN'S FINCH ♀ ♂

175. HOUSE FINCH ♂ ♀

176. LAZULI BUNTING ♂ ♀

177. RED CROSSBILL ♀ ♂

Rosinds Holmes

79. AMERICAN GOLDFINCH

180. LESSER GOLDFINCH

178. PINE SISKIN

181. LAWRENCE'S GOLDFINCH

183. RUFOUS-SIDED TOWHEE

182. GREEN-TAILED TOWHEE

184. BROWN TOWHEE

INDEX